EMOTION

YOUR PASSPORT TO CONFIDENCE

Willia H. Glover, Ph.D.

EQ POWER COACHING, INC.

Copyright © 2015 by Willia Glover

All rights reserved.
No part of this book may be photocopied or otherwise
reproduced without written permission
from the author.

EQ Power Coaching, Inc.
eqpower@comcast.net

ISBN: 978-0-9908225-0-9

Cover Design: Jina Lee, Little Bear Art & Design
Colorado Springs, Colorado

Interior Design: The Publishing Pro LLC,
Colorado Springs, Colorado

To Mai,
my deepest love and gratitude
for your unwavering
belief in me.

Contents

Preface	vii
Introduction	1
Chapter 1: It Started in School	3
Chapter 2: Deflated Self-Esteem	9
Chapter 3: Socially Defined Identity	14
Chapter 4: Not Heard and Invisible	18
Chapter 5: Resurrected Emotion	23
Chapter 6: Humiliated at Work	28
Chapter 7: Male or Female as Leader	35
Chapter 8: Feeling Rejected	40
Chapter 9: Emotions Inform and Empower	45
Chapter 10: Uncover and Overcome Emotional Obstacles	51
Selective Reading	55

Preface

Humans—we are first and foremost emotional beings. As newborns, we cry to get our needs met because emotion is our only form of communication. As a result, our emotional capabilities develop long before the rational mind. Given this developmental process in newborns, one can surmise that humans are quite adept at dealing with their emotions. Surprisingly, this is often not the case.

Emotions activate a wide range of feelings that we categorize as glad, mad, sad, or scared. However, I am interested in only those emotions that make me feel sad, mad, or scared.

These emotions trigger intense anxiety and emotional pain. They disrupt productivity and take control of my thoughts for hours, days, and even years. They leave deep wounds that I rarely mention to others. This type of emotion manifests itself as a piercing visceral feeling that demands an immediate response.

I am personally familiar with the power of these intense emotions, but not until my study of emotions in the workplace did I learn about their impact upon others.

During the study, I interviewed several female executives. Each participant was to recount an emotionally stressful experience at work. One interview was particularly enlightening.

This participant and her corporate executive persona immediately intrigued me. I listened intently as she shared her story in a rather impersonal tone with polished professionalism. I watched, also, in astonishment as her face reddened with emotion. Her vocal expression was telling part of the story while her body was revealing the rest of the story. Surprised by her body's reaction to her experience, I assumed that it was a recent occurrence. After she finished her story, I asked, "Did this happen recently?" In a calm and detached manner she responded, "No, this happened four or five years ago." My body quivered.

Although she was a person of power and influence in the workplace, managing intense emotions was still a challenge for this executive. This was proof that I was not the only person challenged by these emotions. This new insight gave me the courage I needed to share my emotional journey with others.

I thought that repressing these intense emotions was the best way to manage them. It helped me eliminate the anxiety and stress I felt. I have learned, however, that repressing my emotions is what causes suffering and keeps me stuck functioning below my potential. Instead of repressing my emotions as I once did, I have learned to pay attention to them and what they are telling me about myself. Doing so eliminates anxiety and releases me from emotional bondage.

I think of these emotions as carriers of critical information specifically designed for me. Instead of instinctively repressing them, I am now curious about what they are trying to tell me. Initially, it required a lot of effort for me to access the message. However, the process of decoding the message without succumbing to the emotion has gotten much easier.

The benefits of exposing and eliminating emotional barriers that impede personal and professional growth are invaluable. Emotions are the key to revealing these barriers and the first step toward getting unstuck.

Acknowledgments

Endless thanks to my Sisters of the Yam—Kathie Elzie, Delma Johnson, and Betty Shepard. Your loving friendship was a source of encouragement and motivation.

I will always be grateful for your insightful and supportive feedback throughout this birthing process.

*An intense emotion
is a defense mechanism
that is triggered
when opposing beliefs collide*

Introduction

I am about to share with you my journey from emotional bondage to emotional healing and renewed self-confidence. In the following chapters, I share several of my most intense and painful emotional experiences. Each chapter describes the precipitating interaction, the emotional wounding caused by it, and the approach I used to restore my self-esteem and confidence.

As a youngster, I learned through social conditioning to control my feelings. I often heard expressions such as:

- "Little girls are like sugar and spice and everything nice";
- "Don't let them see you cry";
- "Little girls don't get angry"; and
- "Little boys don't cry."

When I entered the workplace, I was told to "leave my emotions at the door." The belief is that organizations are systems of rational thought with little tolerance for emotions.

Taking the advice of my elders and business savvy coworkers, I became competent at ignoring and repressing stressful emotions. It helped to eliminate my anxiety and made it easier for me to function more effectively—or so I thought.

As a consequence, I unknowingly programmed myself to avoid experiences that could possibly cause emotional pain. While I avoided emotional pain, I also relinquished my capability to make conscious choices. Much like a computer program operating in the background, my repressed emotions controlled every choice I made. This created a continuing pattern of self-sabotage that lasted for years.

I have since learned that an intense emotion is a signal that my conscious and unconscious thoughts are not aligned. When my conscious thought is out of alignment with my unconscious belief, my unconscious mind controls my actions and creates the perfect condition for anxiety and internal conflict.

Emotion is an integral part of every rational decision. There is a feeling attached to every choice. Emotions are far more important in decision-making than rational thought.

If I repress an intense feeling without exploring it, I am destined for emotional bondage. Choosing to explore them instead provides a tremendous source of information and empowerment.

CHAPTER 1

It Started in School

I was born and raised in the southeastern part of the United States. I spent my summers playing marbles, jacks, and climbing the persimmon tree in my backyard. I felt nurtured by my family, teachers, and small community.

The summer after I finished the fifth grade, my family and I moved to Chicago. It was here that my way of being in the world changed.

When I enrolled in school, my parents learned that I would need to repeat the fifth grade. The school administrator assumed that my southern education had not prepared me for the sixth grade in Chicago. As a result, I started the school year as a fifth grader. However, within six weeks my teacher determined that my skills were comparable to those of the average sixth grader and I moved to the sixth-grade class. This is where my earliest memory of an intense emotional experience occurred.

❦

My class is participating in the school's annual science fair. Each student is to create a science project and demonstrate it at the fair.

My project includes the use of a balloon. Although this word is in my science book, I don't know how to pronounce it. Checking the dictionary, I discover that the word is composed of two syllables and the letter "l" precedes and follows a hyphen. Using the syllables to help me, I conclude that it is pronounced bal-loon (the first syllable rhyming with "pal"), not bah-loon or buh-loon.

The day of the science fair arrives. I am delighted to be demonstrating my project to students from other classes. Things are going well until a few of my classmates stop by my station to observe my demonstration. I say the word *bal-loon* several times, as I describe my project to them. First, I hear snickers and then someone shouts, "buh-loon!" Suddenly, I realize that I have mispronounced the word *balloon* the entire afternoon. My mood quickly shifts from feeling confident to feeling stupid.

While I dismantle my project, my classmates entertain themselves by mocking the way I pronounced *balloon*, complete with a southern accent. I pretend to be untouched by their comments, but I am deeply embarrassed and humiliated.

As I walk home from school, I can only think about how I humiliated myself in front of all the students in my new school. Disappointed with myself, I wonder if the school administrator was correct about my not being prepared for the sixth grade. I don't want others to know how ashamed I am, nor do I want to discuss my feelings with anyone, not even my parents. What I want most of all is for the memory to go away. Instead, my mind repeatedly returns to the experience and the painful feelings associated with it.

THE WOUNDING

I thrived in school when I lived in the South. My teachers encouraged and nurtured my interest in learning. Learning was a game of exploration. I could ask questions, provide incorrect answers, and ask more questions until I fully understood a concept. Learning was enjoyable.

In Chicago, however, I received a reprimand for giving the wrong answer or doing something incorrectly. I cringed at the thought of volunteering an answer in the classroom unless I was certain it was correct.

I learned to repress my hurt feelings because my budding self-esteem as a sixth grader was not strong enough to defend itself. Doing so, however, adversely affected my self-esteem and confidence. I retreated into the shadows of emotional safety and avoided experiences that exposed me to the possibility of ridicule. Instead of blossoming with each experience, I settled for just existing.

Learning about the power of emotions helped me recognize how my need for emotional safety influenced the choices I made. It took decades to realize how profoundly the bal-loon experience—and others like it—had affected me.

The Healing

This section in each of the following chapters demonstrates how I used my emotions to expose hidden emotional barriers and initiate emotional healing.

Relying upon my emotional intelligence training,

I created a simple five-step process for uncovering and overcoming invisible barriers to growth. I applied this process to each of my emotional episodes and recorded what I discovered in this section of each of the succeeding chapters. Below are insights from the emotional episode in this chapter.

Step 1—Clearly identify my emotion. Does it make me feel sad, mad, or scared?

In this instance, I was certain that I did not feel sad. However, I was not clear about whether I was mad or scared. Once it was clear to me that I was scared, I focused on clarifying the fear.

Step 2—What am I sad about, mad about, or scared of?

I was afraid of being ridiculed, rejected, and called a dummy by my classmates.

Step 3—What is my unconscious belief? (What are my feelings telling me about myself?)

In the past, this is where I would repress my emotion. It was critical that I eliminate the emotional pain and not think about the experience anymore. This time, however, I chose not to repress the emotion, but explore it instead.

What was this emotion saying about me? What was

the unconscious belief that controlled my behavior?

My unconscious belief was that because I grew up in the South, I was not as smart as my classmates in Chicago.

I did not want to believe this was true, but it certainly appeared to be.

Step 4—Test the validity of my belief. (What evidence is there to support this self-limiting belief?)

I had no evidence to support this belief.

The fact that I was finally in the sixth grade indicated that my fifth-grade teacher and school administrator were convinced that I was just as capable as the average sixth grader in Chicago.

Step 5—Replace the old belief with a new one based upon a more accurate assessment of what is true for me.

My new belief: Given that I successfully met the academic requirements of my sixth-grade class proves that I am just as intelligent as my peers in Chicago.

CHAPTER 2

Deflated Self-Esteem

Although I lived within two blocks of a college prep high school, I attended a vocational high school several miles from home. My parents believed it was more important for me to learn skills that would lead to employment after high school. I had the following experience during my senior year.

I am looking forward to the senior prom and the graduation ceremony. My goal after high school is to obtain a job as a secretary and earn more than I do now as a part-time typist. During a trip to my locker, I overhear a couple of students talking about going to college. Suddenly, I have a new goal. Although I know nothing about college and my vocational training has not prepared me for college,

I am sure that I want to go there.

Intrigued by the prospect of going to college, I make an appointment to talk with my high school counselor right away. Previous conversations with my counselor have always been informative and inspiring. I am confident that she will provide the information I need to put me on the path to college.

I tell my counselor that I heard others talk about going to college and realize that this is what I want too. My counselor turns to her file cabinet and pulls out my Scholastic Aptitude Test (SAT) scores. Without considering that I am an honor student and editor of the school newspaper, she looks at me and says, "You are not college material."

As I struggle to understand what I heard, I sit speechless waiting for some sign of hope. The silence is deafening. Crushed emotionally and feeling dejected, I leave her office thinking that going to college is simply beyond the realm of possibility for me and it was foolish of me to think that it was possible. In that moment, I make the decision to confine future goals to only those I know I can achieve.

The Wounding

It was extremely painful to hear that I did not possess the intelligence required to enter college. Again, I thought that I was not as capable as my peers were and, therefore, inferior in some way. I felt ashamed, hopeless, and powerless because I could not obtain something I truly wanted.

With my hope deflated, I gave up wishing for things I could never have. It was my way of protecting me from disappointment. Hiding in the shadow of emotional safety became a reliable survival strategy. It protected me from emotional pain, but it also laid the foundation for unwanted self-sabotage, which reinforced my fears. My fear of disappointment and sense of inferiority adversely influenced my self-esteem and confidence.

Although my chance for getting into college had been quashed, my interest in college had not been completely abandoned. While working as a full-time secretary, the desire to attend college reemerged. This time I applied for admission to a local junior college and was delightfully surprised when I was accepted. After junior college, I focused my attention on an undergraduate degree in education. Years later, I became interested in the way organizations function and how to design work environments in which the employees and the organization could thrive. Eventually, I earned a master's degree in human resources and a doctoral degree in human and organizational systems.

As I was receiving my Ph.D. degree, I remember thinking—if only my high school counselor could see me now.

THE HEALING

Step 1—Clearly identify my emotion. Does it make me feel sad, mad, or scared?

I was scared.

Step 2—What am I sad about, mad about, or scared of?

I was afraid or being rejected and disappointed.

Step 3—What is my unconscious belief? (What are my feelings telling me about myself?)

I did not have the level of intelligence necessary for college.

Step 4—Test the validity of my belief. (What evidence is there to support this self-limiting belief?)

I had no evidence to support this belief.

A member of the National Honor Society, editor of the school newspaper, and candidate for a high school diploma were clear indicators of my ability to meet the requirements of college admission.

Step 5—Replace the old belief with a new one based upon a more accurate assessment of what is true for me.

My new belief: I am, without a doubt, "college material".

CHAPTER 3

Socially Defined Identity

The episode below happened shortly after I was married. I went into a small boutique where I had an account. When I entered the shop, I was in a good mood and feeling well. By the time I left the store, my mood had changed dramatically.

I am checking out, the clerk informs me that it is time to update my contact information. She asks if I have changed my name, address, or phone number. Being a blissful new bride, I am happy to give her my new name. Afterwards, she says, "I need to ask a few questions about your husband. What is his name, and where does he work?"

The clerk's sudden and probing interest in

my husband, who has no account at this shop, is annoying. My response is: "Listen, this is my account, not my husband's. Furthermore, he will probably never come into this store."

She looks up at me and calmly replies, "I understand, Ma'am. Now, what is your husband's full name and where does your husband work?"

Reluctantly, I provide the information requested and leave the shop. I sense that something deeply personal is taken from me. With the mention of three simple letters—m-r-s—my identity is fundamentally altered.

The Wounding

I was bewildered both by my brief interaction with the clerk and the deep sense of loss I felt. The clerk's questioning seemed to discount me as a responsible account holder and ignored me as a person. Every question threatened my sense of identity and independence.

I had recently earned an undergraduate degree in education. I was employed as a full-time teacher and financially supporting myself. The thought that I was not capable of managing my financial needs insulted my sense of independence. I was angry.

My response to the interaction with the store clerk was a prediction of what was to become a reality for me.

Within a year, my husband was transferred to a military base in another state. I was unable to find full-time work as a teacher because of my out-of-state certification. Without an income, I became a dependent. As a result, I experienced a significant shift in my self-perception that affected every choice I made. I found myself seeking approval from and deferring to others. My needs and desires were no longer a priority.

As I thought about the feelings triggered by the store clerk and made evident with our relocation, I realized that beneath it all I feared the loss of my identity as an independent being.

The Healing

Step 1—Clearly identify my emotion. Does it make me feel sad, mad, or scared?

I was mad.

Step 2—What am I sad about, mad about, or scared of?

I was afraid or being stereotyped as a financial dependent.

I was infuriated about feeling dismissed by the store clerk as a reliable account holder.

Step 3—What is my unconscious belief? (What are my feelings telling me about myself?)

I believed that as a married woman, business owners considered me an unreliable account holder.

Step 4—Test the validity of my belief. (What evidence is there to support this self-limiting belief?)

I had no supporting evidence to justify my belief.

My account had not been overdue and I had never missed a payment. I had not defaulted on my account and I was employed full-time.

Step 5—Replace the old belief with a new one based upon a more accurate assessment of what is true for me.

My new belief: I am a reliable account holder and I make responsible spending decisions.

CHAPTER 4

Not Heard and Invisible

This emotional episode occurred during a community forum where men and women from the community gathered to provide input on several community related issues. I was one of those invited to participate.

We are sitting along both sides of a rectangular table. The facilitator is sitting to my left at the head of the table.

During the meeting, the facilitator asks each participant to comment on a particular issue. When it is my turn to respond, I do so with a suggestion. The facilitator simply nods and continues on to the next person.

Initially, I think her failure to acknowledge my suggestion is because it will not be easy to implement in our community. However, as the facilitator continues around the table to the third person after me, I begin to have doubts. The third person happens to be a male.

Although stated somewhat differently, he makes the same suggestion that I made minutes earlier. This time the facilitator expresses excitement about the suggestion and praises the participant for his valuable contribution. Why did the facilitator acknowledge his response and not mine?

My mind struggles to make sense of what is happening. Is it because I am a stay-at-home mom, unlike the other professionals in the room? Is there something about me as the messenger? Can it be that the suggestion sounded more erudite coming from a male?

Regardless, I am annoyed. I feel like the invisible person in the room.

I don't know how to respond without expressing my irritation with the process and the facilitator. I am afraid others will think that I am "too sensitive" or "taking things too personally." So, I say nothing.

The Wounding

I did not feel heard or valued as an invited participant. I sensed that my contribution had less value than that of other participants. I felt rejected once again and memories of old wounds surfaced immediately.

While reliving this experience, I made a disturbing discovery—my self-perception and self-worth were linked to being employed.

As a stay-at-home mom who had been out of the workforce for several years, I lost my sense of independence. That loss manifested as low self-esteem and self-doubt. Did I unknowingly communicate my unconscious belief that as a stay-at-home mom I had nothing of value to contribute to the forum?

This is a good example of how my repressed emotions lead to the development of self-limiting beliefs. I could have spared myself considerable suffering if I had the ability to examine my feelings and search for the underlying message within each emotional experience.

The Healing

Step 1—Clearly identify the emotion. Does it make me feel sad, mad, or scared?

I was mad.

Step 2—What am I sad about, mad about, or scared of?

I was agitated about having my voice ignored and having been treated as if I was invisible.

Step 3—What is my unconscious belief? (What are my feelings telling me about myself?)

If unemployed, I had no value. Therefore, my thoughts had no value.

Step 4—Test the validity of my belief. (What evidence is there to support this self-limiting belief?)

I had none.

Although the suggestion I offered was not acknowledged when initially stated, it was applauded when voiced by another participant.

Step 5—Replace the old belief with a new one based upon a more accurate assessment of what is true for me.

My new belief: The value of my thoughts is determined by how I use that knowledge, not my current employment status.

CHAPTER 5

Resurrected Emotion

My mother asked me to help her complete a vital records form. The form asked for her mother's age and date of birth. My mother's response to the questions was, "I don't know." I was stunned by her response and saddened to realize there was much she did not know about her mother. How is it possible that my mother does not know the age and birth date of her parents?

Puzzled by my mother's lack of information about her parents and realizing that I knew nothing about my grandmother's past, I decided to make a special trip and ask her to tell me about her life.

On the drive to my grandparents' home in North Carolina, I envisioned myself peacefully swaying in the swing on their front porch, captivated by the stories of their younger lives. Upon arrival, my grandparents were delighted to see me and greeted me with loving hugs. We talked about how much I had changed and laughed about the things I did as a child.

By the third day of my visit, all of their questions about my parents, my siblings, and me were answered.

The house is quiet. My grandmother and I are alone. It is the perfect time to talk. As I follow her into the kitchen, I am excited about what I am about to learn from our conversation. I say to her, "Grandma, tell me what life was like when you were growing up."

She stops abruptly, spins around, and stares into my eyes with a glare that pierces the core of my being and shouts, "Don't you ever ask me that again!" Then she turns and walks away. End of discussion.

Deeply wounded, by the tone of her response, I struggle to hold back my tears. I don't know why my seemingly harmless question triggered such anger.

On the drive home, I relived that moment repeatedly trying to understand my grandmother's reaction to my question.

A decade or so later, I am invited to attend a community race-relations workshop. I am married and the mother of two young children. We live in a small community outside of Richmond, Virginia. The day before the workshop, trying to reassure myself that I could participate in a rational discussion about race relations without becoming emotional, I said to myself, "I can handle this."

The session starts at 9 A.M. on Saturday at the local community center. I am feeling well and looking forward to an engaging and meaningful discussion.

By 11 A.M. I sense a dramatic shift in the way I feel. This is disturbing because I am not aware of anything that could evoke such a shift in my mood.

My body is flooded with a sense of agony, helplessness, and despair. It is a visceral connection to the traumatic experiences of my ancestors. I cannot control or repress my feelings. The emotion is so overwhelming I want to holler.

However, as I open my mouth, I find that I have no voice. My emotions have taken control of my mind and body. I can't express what is happening to me. Finally, I understand my grandmother's reaction to my question.

REFLECTIONS

Unlike previous emotional episodes where I was the protagonist, this was my first adventure as an emotional conduit. This episode was not about my personal experience, but I felt the excruciating emotion as if I actually experienced it. Thus, these comments do not follow *The Wounding/The Healing* structure of other chapters.

I suspect that my grandmother's childhood was so traumatic that when she became an adult and started her own family, she buried her past. Except the names of her siblings and parents, nothing about her past was ever shared with her children.

With her siblings living in other regions of the country and deceased parents, I suppose it was easier to bury her past and start anew. Although my grandmother's memory of childhood traumas was concealed, it was never deleted. It remained dormant in her body as it was passed down to and through her offspring.

It appeared as though my grandmother's efforts to obliterate the memories of her past had succeeded until my question reconnected her to those experiences and the crippling emotions attached to them.

This gripping experience connected me to my grandmother's aversion of her childhood memories and explained why my mother knew so little about her. My soul ached.

CHAPTER 6

Humiliated at Work

This episode occurred while employed as department secretary for a company in Richmond, Virginia.

It is 8:30 A.M., and I am sitting at my desk in the hall outside the offices of the members of my department. It is common for my coworkers to assemble in front of my desk each morning to sip coffee and exchange small talk. Although my desk serves as a place to congregate and chat, I am not always an active participant.

While my coworkers engage in the routine morning exchange, the general manager of the company bounds toward them on the way to his office. He stops suddenly for a brief chat. I notice that he has a sheet of paper in his hand. As he interacts with my coworkers, he crumples the sheet of paper in his hand as if he is preparing to toss it into the wastebasket. I think nothing of it and turn my attention to something on my desk.

Then, a wad of paper strikes my forearm. My coworkers laugh. While I was startled and stunned, I was not amused. The general manager walks away and my coworkers head toward their offices, still laughing.

Initially, I feel humiliated but my feelings quickly shift to outright anger. Within moments, my brain shuts down and my emotions take over. I try to focus on my work, but I can think of nothing except how I feel about being struck with a wad of paper thrown by the general manager of the company.

I am a heartbeat away from tears and so distracted by the intense feelings that I can't sit calmly at my desk. I feel compelled to seek a place of refuge so that I can compose myself. I don't want anyone to ask, "Are you okay?" because I am not okay.

In search of privacy, I rush to the restroom

around the corner. I need to be able to hear myself think. This incident has changed the course of my entire day. How am I going to respond?

By the time I emerge from the restroom, I realize that I must talk with the general manager about humiliating me in the presence of my coworkers. I am fully aware that confronting the general manager might mean that I will be fired, but every fiber in my body is urging me to do just that. Before bolting down the hall to his office, I sit at my desk and seriously consider this action.

Overcome with anger, I am also intimidated by the general manager and his power. I decide it would be wise to have a coworker accompany me as a witness. I ask a female coworker who witnessed the incident and with whom I had a good rapport to accompany me. She refuses without hesitation. Disappointed and worried that I might have to do this alone, I return to my desk to rethink my options. Determined to have this conversation with the general manager, I approach another coworker, whose job it is to accompany employees to meetings with their superiors. She agrees to accompany me, and we go directly to the general manager's office.

He is alone and invites us to come in and sit down. I can't sit. I am feeling too anxious and angry. Instead, I stand at the side of his huge desk to capture his complete attention.

"What can I do for you?" he asks. It is an obvious question, but I am so overcome with anger that I don't respond to it. Instead, I blurt out, "I am appalled that a man of your stature would behave the way you just did with me."

He quickly responds with, "What do you want me to do, say I'm sorry?"

Agitated by the tone of his response, I say, "No. What you did is unbecoming of a man in your position and you don't know me that well. Don't do that again!" I turn and walk quickly out of his office, as my coworker follows. Shaking uncontrollably, I thank her for supporting me and return to my desk.

I am certain there will be repercussions. Preparing for the worse, I gather my things, place them in the bottom drawer of my desk, and wait to be escorted out of the building. Time passes, and it gets close to lunchtime. Still, no one has approached me.

I work until the end of the workday feeling

anxious all the while. No one comes to fire me. I still have my job.

Since that encounter, the general manager never passes my desk without a friendly greeting.

THE WOUNDING

As I reflect upon that moment now, I believe that the general manager was trying to be playful but did so in an awkward and unprofessional way. At the time of this incident, I believed that the general manager was illustrating his skill at taunting less powerful employees. The general manager had a reputation for publicly berating subordinates. As the lowest ranking employee in my department and one of the least powerful employees in the company, I instinctively assumed ill intent on his behalf. His behavior reminded me of how it feels to be powerless and humiliated.

Nevertheless, I was determined to express to him my disapproval of his behavior.

Although hijacked by my anger, I composed myself long enough to assess my feelings and made a decision about how I wanted to respond. My response was nothing more than a knee-jerk reaction to a powerful internal drive to protect my dignity. The adrenaline inherent in emotional energy compelled me to act.

Beyond telling the general manager that I disapproved of his behavior, I never thought about a desired outcome. I expected to lose my job; however, that was not my intent. My intent was to express to him my disapproval of his behavior. Driven by my anger and fear, somehow I chose to respond in a way that affirmed my sense of self.

THE HEALING

Step 1—Clearly identify the emotion. Does it make me feel sad, mad, or scared?

I was mad.

Step 2—What am I sad about, mad about, or scared of?

I was angry about being the target of entertainment for my co-workers.

Step 3—What is my unconscious belief? (What are my feelings telling me about myself?)

As a secretary, female, and African-American, I don't command the respect that my co-workers do.

Step 4—Test the validity of my belief. (What evidence is there to support this self-limiting belief?)

I was well respected as the secretary for my department by all those who interacted with our staff, including the general manager's executive assistant. Thus, I had no evidence to support my belief.

Step 5—Replace the old belief with a new one based upon a more accurate assessment of what is true for me.

My new belief: Regardless of my job, gender, or ethnicity, I am entitled to the same professional courtesy from the general manager as any other employee of the company.

CHAPTER 7

Male or Female as Leader

This incident occurred the first day of a leadership development program. Participants are asked to form teams according to assigned numbers in preparation for a timed learning exercise. There are four females and one male on our team, none of whom know each other.

The facilitator explains the exercise and appoints a leader for each team. I am appointed leader of our group. Typically more comfortable as a follower, I agree to accept this role because, after all, it is a leadership development workshop.

As the timed exercise begins, a shift in leadership is already taking place. I don't become aware of it, however, until later. As we start to create our problem-solving strategy, I notice that the female team members defer to the one male on our team instead of actively voicing their own ideas. I wonder if they think our male colleague has more experience at solving this type of problem than anyone on our team.

Remembering that this is a timed exercise, I put this concern aside and return my attention to collaboratively designing a team strategy. Once our strategy is drafted, I ask my team members to voice their objections. No one has an objection.

Now, we must rehearse the strategy in preparation for our presentation to the entire class. I take the lead with the presentation and ask the other team members to follow in the sequence outlined in our strategy. However, when it is time for the next team member to present, no one comes forward. As I signal to the next person to present, I notice the bewildered look on my teammates' faces. It is as if they have no clue as to what we are doing.

Seizing the moment, the male member interjects a completely new strategy. Immediately, the other three women accept the new strategy without questions or comments. Suddenly, our team has a new leader.

As our new leader steps into his role, it becomes clear that my leadership is the victim of sabotage. Recognizing that my authority has been usurped and that we are rapidly running out of time, I acquiesce.

The Wounding

I was appointed team leader by the workshop facilitator. I felt betrayed and abandoned when the team rejected my leadership during the rehearsal of our agreed upon strategy. The absence of support was acutely unnerving. I could not help but think that my team's action was in response to something they disliked about me, but I did not have the courage to ask if my assumption was accurate.

Doubts surfaced about my ability to lead and whether I, as an African American female, would be accepted as a leader. As in the past, I quickly repressed those thoughts and uncomfortable feelings so that I could continue to function. Led by our new leader, we made our presentation as a team and completed the exercise.

After feeling rejected as an appointed team leader, I avoided volunteering for or accepting any team leadership role for the remainder of the program. I knew I was sabotaging myself, but emotional safety had suddenly become my top priority.

Later, it occurred to me that the behavior of the women on my team had nothing to do with me personally. I sensed that it was a reflection of a socially conditioned belief that men are better at problem solving and leadership than women are although the women outnumbered the men in this program.

After more thought, I realized that I, too, shared the same conditioned belief that contributed to reinforcing my self-doubt.

To experience rejection was and still is a challenge; however, I no longer internalize and identify with it.

The Healing

Step 1—Clearly identify the emotion. Does it make me feel sad, mad, or scared?

I was mad.

Step 2—What am I sad about, mad about, or scared of?

I was upset because once again I had been rejected, but this time I didn't know why.

Step 3—What is my unconscious belief? (What are my feelings telling me about myself?)

I didn't have the ability to be an effective leader.

Step 4—Test the validity of my belief. (What evidence is there to support this self-limiting belief?)

Although I was rejected as team leader, I had no proof that I was incapable of being an effective leader.

Step 5—Replace the old belief with a new one based upon a more accurate assessment of what is true for me.

My new belief: During my brief tenure as team leader, I demonstrated good participatory leadership skills (inclusive, active listening, group oriented goal setting and achievement).

I am certainly capable of being an effective leader.

CHAPTER 8

Feeling Rejected

After a full day of teamwork and experiential exercises, our group reconvened for a special evening presentation.

I park my car in the underground garage and take the elevator up to the conference room. As I enter the conference room, I pass Jordan who is leaving. Jordan is one of my colleagues. As usual, I say, "Hi, Jordan, how are you?" I am surprised when he says nothing because he usually returns my greeting. I thought, "Huh, that's not like Jordan. Why didn't he say something?"

I dismiss the thought and walk over to three female colleagues standing near the door. Consciously making eye contact with each person I say, "Hi, Ladies, how are you?" For the second time, no one acknowledges my greeting. Immediately, I think that my colleagues are publicly shunning me and everyone in the room is witnessing it. This is perplexing and humiliating.

Usually I am not concerned when someone does not return my greeting, especially if I don't know the person. But I know these people. We have been in this program together for nine months and interacting with each other all day today.

I feel sick to my stomach. My heart is beating faster. I am feeling flushed around my face and throat. I want to cry. I want to get out of this room as quickly as possible without drawing attention to myself.

I walk quickly out of the room into the hall and sprint the rest of the way to the restroom. By the time I reach the stall, I am gasping for breath. Tears are gushing down my cheeks. I barricade myself inside the stall and snatch wads of toilet paper from the roll to trap my tears before they wet my blouse. I am infuriated with myself because I am unable to control the uncomfortable feelings.

It takes several minutes to regain my composure. I go back to the conference room determined to find out why my classmates did not say hello to me. I approach Jordan and say, "Hi, Jordan. I spoke to you earlier and you didn't respond. What was that about?" His response is simply, "I didn't see you; I'm sorry."

A question emerges, "We were close enough to touch each other. How could you not see me?" Continuing on my quest, I approach one of the women I spoke to earlier and ask the same question.

Her response is, "I don't know why I didn't say hello. I don't have an excuse." I am speechless and cannot believe I went through this gut-wrenching ordeal for nothing.

THE WOUNDING

I was relieved to learn that I had done nothing to justify my colleagues' response to my greeting. Nevertheless, it was disturbing to realize that my colleagues had the power to wreak havoc with my emotions. More important, I was annoyed with myself for not being able to control this distressing emotion.

Aware that I didn't have the skills required to solve this problem alone, I sought help. I started with a spiritual counselor who suggested that I research the term emotional intelligence that surfaced during one of my sessions. While researching this term, I discovered, luckily, an emotional intelligence workshop in my local area. Excited about having ready access to training that directly related to my problem, I signed up and started my journey toward emotional awareness and understanding.

THE HEALING

Step 1—Clearly identify my emotion. Does it make me feel sad, mad, or scared?

I was scared.

Step 2—What am I sad about, mad about, or scared of?

Again, I was afraid of being rejected by my colleagues.

Step 3—What is my unconscious belief? (What are my feelings telling me about myself?)

I was not an equal peer to others in this program because I was not an active member of the workforce.

Step 4—Test the validity of my belief. (What evidence is there to support this self-limiting belief?)

Although I was not actively employed with some business or organization like most of my colleagues, I had no evidence to support this belief.

Step 5—Replace the old belief with a new one based upon a more accurate assessment of what is true for me.

My new belief: Like all candidates, I had to satisfy the requirements for admission to this program. Employment was not one of the prerequisites. Thus, I was completely qualified to be there and I belonged there. This emotionally taxing experience was the catalyst that launched my search to explain why I was having these intense emotional episodes and how to manage them more effectively.

CHAPTER 9

Emotions Inform and Empower

After completing the basic emotional intelligence program, I enrolled in the Emotional Intelligence at Work certification program. I was intrigued with the topic and eager to become a practitioner. With my new knowledge of emotions, I was confident that I could effectively manage future emotional episodes in my life.

After the program ended, however, I had another emotionally challenging experience. This one clearly demonstrated that resolving my own issues would be much more challenging than I anticipated.

Determined to solve my problem with emotions, I sought help from a variety of other sources—personal development workshops, personal growth writings, personal retreats, and metaphysical practitioners. Although each source provided additional insight, it became evident that focusing solely on the acute emotion was not the path to my answer. I would need to dig much deeper to uncover the source of the felt but unexpressed pain of each emotional episode.

As I wrestled with random emotional episodes, I stumbled upon an enlightened discovery. I learned that an intense emotional reaction from me signals a misalignment between a conscious thought and an unconscious belief about myself. When my conscious thought and my unconscious belief are not aligned, any situation that appears to confirm the unconscious belief will ignite internal conflict and trigger an intense emotion. This was the key to understanding my emotional episodes.

This new insight shifted my perception of intense emotions from an integral part of the human experience that I must cope with to that of an untapped source of invaluable information.

Using what I know and understand about emotions, I created an exercise, outlined in Chapter 10, to access this core information and it works!

In this chapter I reveal the unresolved and hidden areas of internal conflict that stunted my growth and kept me stuck in a cyclical pattern of self-doubt and fear. It is in these areas that there was a critical misalignment between a conscious thought about myself and a deeply held false belief. I finally understand the cause of my emotional episodes. That's priceless!

SELF-ESTEEM

When told to repeat the fifth grade, seeds of low self-esteem and incompetence started to germinate. As a result, when ridiculed for failing to pronounce a word correctly, I consciously labeled myself as a failure and accepted this self-perception without questioning its validity.

There is no doubt that I failed to pronounce the word *balloon* correctly, but was that sufficient evidence to prove that I, as a person, was a failure? Without messages to contradict this perception of myself, I unknowingly allowed it to become an invisible barrier. This invisible barrier manifested as low self-esteem and controlled the way I moved through my life for decades.

Once I became a mother, however, something changed. I developed a strong but unacknowledged need to protect my underdeveloped identity. For example, in the paper-toss experience my self-esteem took precedence over my fear. I had no idea how courageous I was. The heightened emotional energy created by a threatened identity was much more powerful than the fear of losing my job.

FEAR OF FAILURE

The threat of failure was enough to evoke self-limiting thoughts that developed over time into an ingrained fear.

I avoided opportunities for growth that threatened to trigger uncomfortable thoughts and feelings. I lowered my expectations of myself. I didn't set goals unless I knew I could achieve them. This was a way to protect myself if things did not turn out as I secretly hoped they would.

My choices were controlled by unconscious false beliefs. The fear of failing and the accompanying self-directed thoughts kept me from trying.

FEAR OF REJECTION

Prior to my first position as a teacher, my world was composed of family and friends with whom I felt comfortable. As a professional in the workplace, my social network expanded and so did my exposure to rejection. I experienced what it felt like to be snubbed, ignored, and excluded. The debilitating thoughts and feelings resulting from these experiences caused me to gravitate towards less threatening one-to-one and small-group encounters.

The habitual behaviors adopted in response to my fears distorted my self-perception and sense of potential. The impact upon my personal growth and development was significant and I regret that I did not know how to respond differently.

Before I learned that unconscious beliefs adopted from my environment dictated my behavior, I was convinced that the other person caused me to feel angry or hurt. Actually, the other person simply pushed one of my "repressed feeling" buttons. This activated the accompanying emotion that produced a knee-jerk reaction.

Repressed emotions encourage reactive and often ineffective behavior. I was conditioned to reacting automatically instead of making a conscious choice to respond voluntarily.

An intense emotion is merely a defense mechanism that is triggered when opposing beliefs collide. It serves as a portal for accessing unconscious beliefs and exposing invisible barriers to personal growth and development.

When the hidden barriers are exposed, options for responding differently become available. Choosing to respond differently means that I can focus on my desired outcome, analyze my response options, and select the one that will most likely help me achieve the desired outcome without guilt, shame, or regret. That is power!

This is not an easy process, however. The excavating of deeply repressed false self-perceptions is a daunting endeavor that requires persistence, time, and patience.

It took me some time to let go of my resistance to probing deeper. Once I uncovered the hidden beliefs responsible for my emotional episodes, I replaced them with beliefs that were more aligned with my true identity. A belief aligned with my true identity has no fear attached to it and is no longer an emotional trigger for me.

The next chapter explains the process used to uncover and overcome invisible barriers to my development and restore my self-esteem and confidence.

CHAPTER 10

Uncover and Overcome Emotional Obstacles

As my personal struggle demonstrates, repressing emotions can lead to years of regret and internal conflict. The objective is to embrace, explore, and allow intense emotions to inform and empower.

Until I knew what my emotional triggers were, I continued to automatically react in emotionally challenging interactions instead of consciously choosing my response. As a consequence, I suffered needlessly.

This chapter describes the five-step process created to uncover and overcome my emotional triggers.

Step 1: Clearly identify my emotion using terms that can be categorized as sad, mad, or scared.

    a. Focus specifically on what I am feeling within my body—not what I am thinking.

b. Ask these questions:
   - What do I really feel?
   - Do I feel sad, mad, or scared?
c. Then, without *any* judgment, simply accept my true feeling as *only a feeling* and nothing more. It helped to write *the feeling* down and say it aloud.

Step 2: What am I sad about, mad about, or scared of?

This step requires that I dig deeper and be specific about why I am sad, angry, or scared.

Step 3: What is my unconscious belief? (What are my feelings telling me about me?)

Ask myself the following questions:
a. What am I trying to avoid?
b. What is it I do not want to feel?
c. In what way do I feel threatened?
d. What is it that frightens me?

Step 4: Test the validity of my fear.
a. Is it real or perceived?

   A stressful response to a real fear usually involves danger to my physical being. If I am not in physical danger, I am most likely responding to a perceived fear—a belief

that something might happen. Most of the stress experienced in our lives today is not in response to imminent physical danger.
b. What evidence is there to justify my belief?
  If I have no evidence to support *my belief*, why should I hold on to *it*?

Step 5: Replace my old belief with a new thought about me that is more accurate.
a. Write it down.
b. Repeat new thought about myself until I *no longer need to.*

Do not repress intense emotions. Connect with them and be curious about what they want you to know. They hold the keys to self-esteem and confidence. Remember, emotions can inform and empower.

What are your emotions trying to tell *you?*

Selected Reading

Allione, Tsultrim. *Feeding Your Demons: Ancient Wisdom for Resolving Inner Conflict.* New York: Little, Brown and Company, 2008.

Ellis, Albert, and Dryden, Windy. *The Practice of Rational Emotive Behavior Therapy.* New York: Springer Publishing Company, 1997.

Gershon, David, and Straub, Gail. *Empowerment: The Art of Creating Your Life As You Want It.* New York: Sterling Publishing Company, 2011.

Glover, Willia. *"Women in Management and Emotional Disequilibrium in the Workplace," Journal of The North American Management Society,* http://mbaa-nams.org/NAMS/JNAMS_files/jnams-vol4-no2-f2009_1.pdf

McLaren, Karla. *The Language of Emotions: What Your Feelings Are Trying to Tell You.* Sounds True, 2010.

Orloff, Judith. *Emotional Freedom: Liberate Yourself From Negative Emotions and Transform Your Life.* New York: Three Rivers Press, 2009.

www.ingramcontent.com/pod-product-compliance
Lightning Source LLC
Chambersburg PA
CBHW031213090426
42736CB00009B/907